The Rhythm of Our Sighs

The Rhythm of Our Sighs

WORDS OF COMFORT FOR
THOSE WHO MOURN

Carol E. Green

ISBN:	Softcover	978-1-4535-7678-6
	eBook	978-1-4990-2260-5

This book was printed in the United States of America.

Rev. date: 06/25/2014

To order additional copies of this book, contact:
Xlibris Corporation
1-888-795-4274
www.Xlibris.com
Orders@Xlibris.com
86079

Contents

CHAPTER III
REMEMBERING AND CELEBRATING

CHAPTER IV
ON THE SIDE OF LIGHT: STARTING TO HEAL

With love and gratitude this book is dedicated in memory of my parents, Dorothy R. and Edmund D. Green

About the Author

Carol E. Green is a United Methodist pastor who has served churches in Missouri and Florida. A significant part of her ministry has been with people who were dying and the family and friends who were grieving. Rev. Green has a B. A. degree in English from Florida Southern College, Lakeland, Florida, and a Master of Divinity Degree from Saint Paul School of Theology, Kansas City, Missouri. Prior to entering the pastoral ministry she taught in a number of different settings. She has two grown children and a grand-daughter. After living most of her life in Florida Carol now lives in Boone, North Carolina.

The author wishes to acknowledge the support and encouragement of:

Peter Bowers, Joy Bowers Barlow, Dr. Connie Green, Cris Stromberg, Gael Wood, Emily Scott, Douglas H. Garwood, Rev. Marianne Romanat, Rev. David McEntire, Rev. Ann R. Hutchens, Rev. Jan Richardson, Carol H. Lewis, Betty Jenkins Blair, Anita Stroupe, Sandy Sisson, The Rev. Dr. Susan Sonnenday Vogel

About the Illustrator

Emily Scott grew up in the beautiful mountains of Boone, North Carolina and studied art at Western Carolina University. She also has a Master's degree in Arts in Health from the University of Glamorgan in Wales. Emily now lives back in western North Carolina with her husband, Andrew, and her young son, George. She enjoys drawing, painting, leading collaborative art projects with community groups, and spending time with her family. She is the niece of the author.

The Rhythm of Our Sighs

In sorrow's circle
Fog obscures the sun.
Minutes elongated
By emptiness
Mark time
Reset by loss.

In sorrow's circle
Memory is golden treasure
And piercing thorn.
In sorrow's circle
Hunger only craves
The lost.
Tears fail to quench
The thirst
For welcome voice.

In sorrow's circle
The silent presence
Of a friend
Says more than word.

In sorrow's circle
God gently moves
To the rhythm of our sighs,
Offering a healing balm,
And tears wiped from our eyes.

"See, the home of God is
among mortals.
He will dwell with them;
they will be his peoples
and God himself will be
with them;
he will wipe every tear from
their eyes.
Death will be no more;
mourning and crying and pain
will be no more,
for the first things have
passed away."

Revelation 21: 3b-4
New Revised Standard Version of the Bible (NRSV)

CHAPTER I

HOW LONG THE ROAD? GRIEVING THE GRADUAL LOSSES

How Long the Road?

Who knows how long the road is
Which you travel now with steps so slow?
Yet, traveling at this new pace
Perhaps there will be time
To see and hear and even feel
Some things you hurried by before.
We do not know why life takes the turns it does—
Why some run right up to the end,
And others jog,
While there are those of us who have to creep and crawl.
But think on this:
Whether we see the sun
Or only shadows,
Whether we dance 'til dawn
Or need bed rest,
As long as there is something we can share,
A smile, a word, a gentle touch,
As long as we can learn,
A game, a name, a new insight from God,
Life still contains a precious cup of sweetness
And an opportunity to praise.

Grieving Before a Death

The process of grieving often begins long before death. Physical and/or mental losses may come very slowly or with unexpected suddenness. No matter what the pace or size of the loss, grieving is a natural response. The person whose body and life is dramatically changing as well as family and close friends all are touched by the loss.

Grief may express itself in angry frustration over not being able to do something she always did for herself. It may come out as tearful agony that the body, once so strong and dependable, has let him down. Spouses or children may feel as if they are being abandoned when heavy new responsibilities replace previous companionship and support.

When the loss includes memory and mental functioning the grief may be as great or greater for the loved ones who watch than for the one experiencing the loss.

Claiming the precious value of what remains is very important. Loss and grief are compounded if the last hours, days and months are spent entirely on grieving what is lost. The gift of time, no matter how short is a resource to treasure. By delighting in each other's presence, rich personalities and shared memories families and friends celebrate their lives. This is the time to express in words, touch and symbols whatever is needed to heal and seal relationships.

Be merciful to me, O God, be merciful to me,
for in you my soul takes refuge;
in the shadow of your wings I will take refuge
Until the destroying storms pass by.
My heart is steadfast, O God.
my heart is steadfast.
I will sing and make melody.
For your steadfast love is as high
as the heavens;
Your faithfulness extends to the clouds.
Psalm 57: 1, 7, 10 NRSV

Flowing Away

As the water flows by me,
I see you flowing away from me.
Now rapidly, then slowly
Drifting to the falls
Where,
One day, there will be
A mighty crash;
And what, if anything,
Remains
Will never be the same.
(Reflection on gradually losing parents)

Holy Wind, Breath of Life, awaken my family and me to your movement in our lives. Sometimes we drift away from placing all our trust in you. We slip into dull resignation and despair. Breathe your Spirit of Power into us, that our faith may be vibrantly active and our trust in You unshakable. Amen.

Slow Losses

I was fearful about slowly losing my parents. Long illnesses and falls had precipitated the deaths of several other family members and people in churches I served. I had seen enough to recognize early signs of significantly declining health and dreaded what might be ahead.

At the same time I trusted God's dependable care. No matter how devastating an illness or destructive a fall, neither my parents nor I could move beyond God's care.

The Lord is my light and my salvation;
Whom shall I fear?
The Lord is the stronghold of my life;
Of whom shall I be afraid?
For he will hide me in his shelter
In the day of trouble;
He will conceal me under the
Cover of his tent;
he will set me high on a rock.
Wait for the Lord;
be strong, and let your heart take courage;
wait for the Lord!
Psalm 27: 1,5,14 NRSV

Waiting

Looking for signs of spring
On a ten degree day in January,
Checking the clock at 9:30 a.m.
On a 9-5 shift,
Planning a graduation party
While still a freshman,
Dreaming of driving
At age eleven,
Staring at the homemade pie
'Til after supper,
Are waiting games
With hopeful, happy goals.

Pacing the waiting room
Of ICU,
Listening for the call
From the doctor's office,
Waiting for lab results,
The minutes are heavy,
And hours are gray.
Tortured by fear,
Almost afraid to hope,
We walk in fog
Preferring not to view
In brightness
What we never want to see.
This is the waiting of another realm.
Words cannot calm the fears
Or lift the fog.
Presence alone can share,
Can jointly bear them.

PM 5:29
12:08 pm

Life in the "Waiting" Room

Waiting for death may involve moments, hours, days, months or years. There may be oasis times when health stabilizes or even improves a little. Hope jumps up, and life goes on until the next relapse, the next complication. Emotions are on a roller coaster. You do not want to rush things. Nevertheless, waiting, with all its unanswered questions and fears, is agony. When thoughts of a decent night's sleep after the struggle is over slip in, you may feel guilty.

Be honest with yourself and those who care about you that waiting is exhausting. Life in the "waiting" room is not a permanent place of residence. Let others share the wait. Allow yourself to rest and to do things that renew you. Treat yourself to a small indulgence. Let laughter into your day.

Give ear to my prayer, O God;
do not hide yourself from my supplication.
My heart is in anguish within me.
the terrors of death have fallen upon me.
Fear and trembling come upon me
and horror overwhelms me.
And I say, "O that I had the wings like a dove!
I would fly away and be at rest;
But I call upon God,
and the Lord will save me.
Evening and morning and at noon
I utter my complaint and moan,
and he will hear my voice.
Psalm 55: 1, 4-6a, 18-19 NRSV

Eternal God, you see us pace away agonizing hours and days. Hear our fear filled questions, "What and When?" As your people waited for release from captivity and relief from oppression and despair, so we also wait now. Waiting makes us restless, irritable, and sometimes even doubtful. Active Spirit, breathe your comfort into all our sighs. Let us feel your death transcending Presence holding us and covering every fear. Amen.

Decisions

Life held in a single syllable,
"Yes" or "No".
How can we decide?
How dare we not?
Her mind is trapped
In a body with no strength.
She weakly nods
As doctors speak.
Their words become the law,
Shackling her
To constant tests, countless procedures,
And endless pain.
We call it "Futile Care."
She knows that death is near.
We also know.
Nurses, chaplains, social workers
All see her fading day by day.
Only the doctors persist
Until we grasp the courage
To say, "No!"
Freeing her to say "good-bye"
And slowly slip away.

End of Life Decisions

End of life decisions can be many and difficult. You may have spent considerable time discussing with your loved one the treatment and care he or she wishes to have when death is near. Nevertheless, even though you have written documents expressing those wishes, making them known can be very painful. Holding firm to the decisions may be an inward and outward battle. It is helpful to have the understanding and support of other members of the care team: family members, close friends, doctors, nurses, chaplains, social workers, hospice workers.

May our struggles and pain remind us, O God, that we are still alive. We have the potential for surprise, for wonder, for learning, for prayer, for witness, yes, and even for hope in the midst of and in spite of suffering. Amen.

What then are we to say about these things? If God is for us, who is against us? He who did not withhold his own Son, but gave him up for all of us, will he not with him also give us everything else? Who will bring any charge against God's elect? It is God who justifies. Who is to condemn? It is Christ Jesus, who died, yes, who was raised, who is at the right hand of God, who indeed intercedes for us. Who will separate us from the love of Christ? Will hardship, or distress, or persecution, or famine, or nakedness, or peril, or sword? As it is written,

"For your sake we are being killed all day long; we are accounted as sheep to be slaughtered." No, in all these things we are more than conquerors through him who loved us. For I am convinced that neither death, nor life, nor angels, nor rulers, nor powers, nor height, nor depth, nor anything else in all creation, will be able to separate us from the love of God in Christ Jesus our Lord.

Romans 8: 31-39

Saying Good-Bye

It's not time yet
But if I wait—
Like a pill swallowed dry
It catches in my throat.

We say it many times in life,
But not for real.
Off to Miss Cornell's class
In plaid and Buster Browns.
"Put my trunk right here, Dad.
I will see you soon."

"Beautiful" "Thank You."
"We'll be back after honeymoon."

A call
And a dream
Three years in between,
My plump, sturdy Dad disappeared.
Doctors hint at what we've feared.
Visits, minutes
Precious time.
The words come hard.
We tremble, "When?"

I love you now.
I'll love you then.
A hug, a prayer,
A strong "Amen".
Through Christ, together

We'll face "When".

(Written for Daddy after his
third surgery in one year.)

Letting Go

All our lives our parents are letting go of us. First they release our hands to let us walk alone. They wave to us at the pre-school or kindergarten door and a few years later reluctantly hand over the car keys. With smiles and tears they say good-bye for a while when we go off to college or away to a job. They see us off when we marry and when we move far away. Their letting go and saying good-bye in many gradual ways helps us to grow and live our own lives. It is also a preparation for the time when we must let them go and say one last good-bye.

How I ached as I wrote this poem for my father, but it was important for both of us. By expressing to him how much I appreciated his walking with me through the many stages of my life and letting me go I also assured him of my willingness to walk with him through this final stage of his life and release him to God.

Jesus Talked of His Death

Jesus' ministry as described in all four Gospels gives us many examples of how Jesus prepared his disciples for the time he would no longer be with them. The disciples had as hard a time as we have with letting go of one they loved.

From that time on, Jesus began to show his disciples that he must go to Jerusalem and undergo great suffering at the hands of the elders and chief priests and scribes, and be killed, and on the third day be raised. And Peter took him aside and began to rebuke him, saying, "God forbid it, Lord! This must never happen to you." But he turned and said to Peter, "Get behind me, Satan! You are a stumbling block for me; for you are setting your mind not on divine things but on human things." Matthew 16: 21-23

The disciples could not yet comprehend the end of the story, but the Christians of the early Church did know about Jesus' death and also about his resurrection. In the midst of death not only from aging and illness but also from violent persecution these Christians, who knew so much about loss and grief, passed on and preserved words of assurance, comfort and hope from the living Christ.

"I will not leave you orphaned; I am coming to you. In a little while the world will no longer see me, but you will see me; because I live, you also will live." John 14: 18-19

"I have said these things to you while I am still with you. But the Advocate, the Holy Spirit, whom the Father will send in my name, will teach you everything, and remind you of all that I have said to you. Peace I leave with you; my peace I give to you. I do not give to you as the world gives. Do not let your hearts be troubled, and do not let them be afraid." John 14: 25-27

Advocate God, you have lived among us and know how hard it is to let go of a loved one. I do not want her to suffer endlessly, but I fear that I will suffer endlessly without this one I love. Still my fears and help me to discern the time to hold on and the time to release her to you. Stand in the great gap she will leave with your limitless comfort and peace. Amen.

Running to Meet

As early as I can remember the story was told and retold. Dorothy Skidmore and Edmund Green were married in Westwood, N.J., November 15, 1942. World War II was already under way, and many had been drafted. Ed was older, 32, so he had hoped he would not have to go. Nevertheless, two weeks before the wedding he got his draft notice. He managed to get some kind of extension until the first of the year, but then he was gone for a long time. There were a few brief visits before he was shipped over to Europe for more than two years. It was an endless time for the newlyweds. They wrote to each other almost every day. Dot carefully saved all of Ed's letters the rest of her life—the evidence of their shining early love.

At last the long distance honeymoon was over. The war was over, and Ed was coming home. They ran, oh, how they ran. Before the train was due Dot left her parent's house running, running up Harrington Avenue and then along the main street, Westwood Avenue. Since the train had arrived a few minutes early and his mother's apartment was two blocks away, Ed ran to greet his mother then ran on the back way down to Harrington Avenue, missing Dot. Moments later they were both running toward each other on Westwood Avenue until they met in a star spangled moment and the rest of their lives began.

The story of "Running to Meet" was a symbol of the urgency and intensity of their love. Most of the rest of their lives was lived far from that urgency and intensity, but the telling and retelling of the story continued to validate their marriage, especially for Dot. She was the one who told most of the family stories. Ed's carefully preserved letters confirm the mutuality of the love and hope with which they began.

The pace and setting were so different when they met again not long ago. It was winter in Boone, N.C. Daddy had died six years earlier in Florida. After Daddy's death Mama had moved to North Carolina near my sister. There, in this town where they had never lived together, they met again with Mama "seeing" Daddy as many "see" loved ones who have died as their own death draws near. With many mixed emotions, we, their daughters, watched them meet.

Dot's feet weren't running anywhere. To take two steps to the commode was more than she could handle. While her tiny, shrunken body lingered on in pain, Dot ran ahead to meet Ed like a young lover again. Gone were the years of complaints and sometimes bitter endurance. When she spoke of their conversations it was with gladness and expectancy. Poignantly she held the pictures of great-grandchildren as if to show them to Ed, the great grandpa who never had a chance to see these little ones.

All of us wondered through the long months of her final, complex illness why she lingered drawing near to death so many times. Much could be said about mistakes made by the doctors and the various attempts at "futile" care. Could it be that this was how long it took her to be ready to see Daddy again? I only know I am grateful that our parents gave my sister and me a final, precious gift, seeing as adults the special love from which we came.

CHAPTER II

GRIEF IS A WOUND: DEATH AND INTENSE GRIEF

Grief Is a Wound

Grief is a wound,
A great, deep wound
Cutting the body,
Bruising emotions and spirit.
At times it bleeds profusely,
Tissue after tissue full of tears.
Then, hidden beneath
Work clothes and a smile
It throbs furiously,
Silently screaming.
Held together by a thread
I function
On automatic pilot
Until the texture of a sweater,
A song on the car radio,
A glimpse of an almost bald head,
The smell of fresh mown grass,
Catches a memory
And my breath.
For a second
Grief was gone
And you were here.
Then I blinked,
And bled once more.
Not wanting to forget,
I fill the empty room
With bittersweet memories
And deep sighs.
Will this gaping, throbbing wound ever heal?

Jesus wept. John 11: 35 KJV

When Mary came where Jesus was and saw him, she knelt at his feet and said to him, "Lord, if you had been here, my brother would not have died." When Jesus saw her weeping, and the Jews who came with her also weeping, he was greatly disturbed in spirit and deeply moved. He said, "Where have you laid him?" They said to him. "Lord, come and see." Jesus began to weep . . . Then Jesus, again greatly disturbed, came to the tomb. It was a cave, and a stone was lying against it. Jesus said, "Take away the stone." . . . So they took away the stone. And Jesus looked upward and said, "Father, I thank you for having heard me. I knew that you always hear me, but I have said this for the sake of the crowd standing here, so that they may believe that you sent me." When he had said this, he cried with a loud voice, "Lazarus, come out!" The dead man came out, his hands and feet bound with strips of cloth, and his face unwrapped in a cloth. Jesus said to them, "Unbind him, and let him go." John 11: 32-35, 38-39a, 41-44

Weeping Jesus, it is comforting to see you with tears like mine. At the death of your friend Lazarus you were moved to weep, to cry in loss and in sympathy for the grieving sisters, Mary and Martha. One who has felt a stream of tears gush forth can both share the well of sorrow and wipe the tears away. Jesus, you released Lazarus from the bonds of death, please release me from the bonds of endless grief. Amen.

It Cannot Be

This poem is in memory of Rodney Eddleman, my first date and my first funeral. His death in August, 1964, started me pondering death and grief. A week after his funeral I went away to college. There was no one who had known Rodney with whom I could share my grief. Even though most of us were away from family and friends and experiencing loss, mourning was not on the agenda in the freshman dorm. Grief needs a voice even if it is decades late.

No!
It cannot be!
Are you sure you heard
The story right?
No!
Next week he will start college.
People our age do not die!
The last time I saw him
Was at our graduation dance.
Drowned—
How could he drown
Trying out skin diving gear
At the beach we all loved?
Gone—
He isn't here any more!
Yesterday
He was phoning friends,
Borrowing his dad's car,
Drinking a Coke.

Today—
There is no today for him.
Will I ever stop expecting
To see him at Bill's Burger,
Downtown,
Or at the beach?
High school football heroes
Grimaced to hold back tears
As they carried his casket to the grave.
I cried and prayed and pondered
Why?
We were friends since sixth grade
When we whispered across the aisle.
In seventh grade he took me to the "prom."
He was my first date
And my first funeral.
How can that be?
Rodney, when death snatched you
It left a wound on me.

Denial

Our minds cannot grasp death at first. Denial is often the immediate response, particularly with a sudden death. We refuse to believe. We try to hear another ending to the story. We may argue with the person trying to tell us the news. We also may argue with the person who has died and with God. The reality of death seems too much to bear. The finality of death is something we do not want to comprehend.

Merciful God, where is your mercy? Light of the World, where are you hiding on this dark day? Living God, how could my friend's life be snatched away? Why must his parents lose all their dreams for him? Assure me somehow that you did not want it to be this way. Amen.

Laments

There are many laments among the psalms. In them we hear the ageless cry to God in times of sorrow and distress. They reassure us that nothing we need to say to God is beyond God's readiness to listen and care. Here is one of many examples:

I cry aloud to God,
Aloud to God, that he may hear me.
In the day of my trouble I seek the Lord;
In the night my hand is
Stretched out without wearying;
my soul refuses to be comforted.
I think of God, and I moan;
I meditate, and my spirit faints.
Has God forgotten to be gracious?
Psalm 77: 1-3, 9a

A few verses later the psalmist remembers the many times God has been gracious and has brought deliverance and hope.

I *will call to mind the deeds of the lord;*
I will remember your wonders of old . . . With your strong arm you redeemed your people,
The descendants of Jacob and Joseph.
Psalm 77: 11, 15

One Snowy Night

The call came about 10:30 p.m.
Many times the call had come.
We had gone to her.
She had stayed.
This was different.
Rehearsing it so many times
Had not eased the pain.
Snow was expected that night,
So was death.
Tiny, delicate flakes were falling
As we entered the nursing home.
For several months
We had watched her body shrink
To this skeleton with skin—
Almost no resemblance to our Mom.
Mom no longer talking wasn't Mom.
She had said her last, "I love you."
We would say just a few more.
The snow was falling harder now,
As we touched her, kissed her,
Waited with her.
All was in readiness.
Blurring the divide of death,
Daddy had "visited" her,
Drawing her into a glad reunion.
Her parents, too, had let her know
They were waiting to welcome her home.
Once more we gave permission,
"It's okay for you to go, Mom.
We will be all right."

There was nothing more to do,
Nothing more to say,
Just to be there with her,
Ready to wave good-bye.
Exhausted, we dozed off briefly
Until the nurse aroused us,
"It is time."
One last "I love you,"
One last kiss,
Until we meet again.
Her shallow breath subsided.
Her heart, much stronger than
Anyone had guessed,
Now rested, too.
With eyes still open
She passed from seeing daughters,
To the sight of long remembered
Loved ones' beckoning smiles.

Hugging each other,
We walked out into
A softly whitened world.
Alone on the road
In the middle of the night,
We, too, were in another realm.
Finished were the hospital vigils.
Gone were the fears
As we answered the phone.
Ended was the helpless watching
As she struggled on in pain.
Silently, the falling snow encircled us.
Tenderly it spread
A soothing salve of peace,
A quiet "Blessed be,"
The long awaited, pure "Amen."

Yes, Relief

After a long illness, or even a short period of intense suffering, relief may closely accompany death. Not only has the person who has died been relieved of suffering; but those who have watched and waited, loved and cared have also been relieved from their emotionally and physically draining vigil. One might say, "How can I feel relieved? My husband/mother/sister/son has just died. I did not want this person to die. Why do I feel relieved?"

While your loved one was dying all your resources were focused on that person. It takes an enormous amount of physical, emotional and spiritual energy to go through what you have just endured. Relief can be a claiming of much needed rest. There will be other intense times in the process of grieving. Accepting relief as a natural response helps people survive the complex process of grieving.

Comfort, O comfort my people,
says your God.
Speak tenderly to Jerusalem,
and cry to her
that she has served her term . . .
He will feed his flock like a shepherd;
He will gather the lambs in his arms,
and carry them in his bosom,
and gently lead the mother sheep.
Isaiah 40: 1-2a, 11

Gently Home

Go gently home,
My friend.
For none will lead you
Down a brighter path
Than One
Who carries you in Mother's arms
With Father's strength of step.
Go gently home,
Dear Friend,
For God who walks with you
Also waits to welcome home
At Glory's door.

Cast your burden on the Lord,
And he will sustain you.
Psalm 55: 22a

Clinging to Hope

Clinging
With aching fingers
Like the last leaf on a tree,
I grasp at hope.
How could you leave me here
Alone?
You are at peace,
"They" say.
I am far from it.
Dull meals
Consumed with Dan Rather and the Evening News
Bear no resemblance to the family table
We once shared.
How many times I open my mouth
To tell you of a mutual friend,
Comment on something I have read,
Ask your opinion,
And the only sound which comes
Is a sob.
You are not there.
Who else would understand?
No one knows our history,
Our unique give and take,
The slant on life
We accepted in each other.

Oh, our lives were not perfect
By any means,
But we knew the feel
Of each other's rough spots,
When to keep silent and
Just the right moment to speak—
At least most of the time.
Going on without you
Is like chipping through the ice
To find firm ground
For each and every step.
I long to walk with ease,
To speak without deep sighs,
To awaken
With the glow of hope.

Feeling Alone

Feeling alone and abandoned by the loved one who has died is part of the process of grief. No one else can fill that particular place in your life. Knowing intellectually that your loved one did not deliberately leave you does not change the sense of abandonment. Even a clear desire not to see the person continue to suffer does not lessen one's own aching loss.

You may experience guilt over the feelings of abandonment because you do not want to place any blame or have any negative thoughts about the one who has died. Recognizing that guilt is another piece of the grief process can free one to acknowledge that the full range of life's emotions are also appropriate to dying and grieving.

While experiencing the loss of a love one, some people may also feel abandoned by God. "Why didn't God intervene? Why didn't God answer prayers for healing? How could God let this happen?" These feelings and questions are both current and ageless. For countless centuries people have cried out to God their anguished questions of life and death. God can handle our most painful and even angry outpourings.

In the midst of grief one may feel spiritually "dry" or seem to be in a spiritual wilderness. In spite of how we may feel God does not abandon us. In ages past when God's people felt abandoned by God, God spoke words of assurance.

But Zion said, "The Lord has forsaken me,
My Lord has forgotten me."
Can a woman forget her nursing child,
Or show no compassion for the child of her womb?
Even these may forget,
yet I will not forget you.
Isaiah 49: 34-35

Comforting One, draw near and hear my sighs. Listen to the echoes of my loneliness. On this solitary path You alone, who knows all sorrows, can meet me and keep me company. Like a hen protecting her chicks, gather me under your wings and guard me from my own despair. Warm me with your peace and nourish me with your healing love. Assure me one more time that you are with me everywhere and always. Amen.

More Than a Butter Dish

I stood in the hall clinging to the butter dish and crying huge, body shaking sobs. Things had gone too far! The butter dish absolutely could not be sold!

It was just a tiny silver-toned tray, but for me it touched the core of many layers of loss and grief. For as long as I could remember it had served as our butter dish for every holiday and special occasion in the family. As I clung to the butter dish I also clung to the many memories stored in every inch of the house that was being cleaned out and sold.

The house on South Twelfth Street in Fort Pierce, Florida, was HOME. My family had moved there the summer before I started seventh grade. Conveniently located halfway between the elementary school and the high school, our house became a gathering place. My sister and I knew that we could bring a friend home from school and there would be iced lemon tea and homemade cookies. Even when Mama was sick and there weren't any cookies, there was always her special iced tea and her interest in any of the day's events we wanted to share.

Living in furnished parsonages most of my adult life and moving frequently, I continued to consider my parents' house as "home." It was a place of continuity for my children as well as for me. We regularly went "home" for a few days after Christmas and Easter and any other time I managed to have a couple of days in a row off to make the trip. Often when we were home Daddy would start the grill and put up the folding ping-pong table that doubled as a picnic table for picnics on the patio.

Seeing how much the children had grown was also a part of most visits. The doorframe into the kitchen was a family growth chart. My parents had measured my sister and me in that spot and each of our children were added to the chart from the time they were old enough to stand and be measured. The cousins compared with each other, and when they each reached about ten they insisted that Grandma and Grandpa be measured also. The race was on to see who would pass parents and grandparents first.

Over the years a few of the furnishings in the house changed, but the feel of that house never changed. We weren't a perfect family. The house held echoes of arguments as well as laughter, stiff silences as well as sweet secrets shared. Yet those walls spelled "love" and "security" to me. Those windows opened onto many dreams.

Even before my father died my mother had broken her hip and had had several little strokes. The three-bedroom house with patio, porch and yard was too much work for them. After Daddy died it quickly became clear to Mama as well as to my sister and me that an apartment in an assisted living facility would be a better living situation for her. So in a six-month period we not only lost Daddy, we also lost "home."

Remnants of that home are scattered now. When I visited my niece at Christmas the lamp from Mama and Daddy's bedroom made her guest room feel familiar. My daughter treasures a green ceramic frog from the porch, and my sister proudly sets her table with the crystal. Mama's rocking chair sits in the living room of my home as a reminder of the old comforts of home. Often I use the treasured butter dish, and sometimes it still brings tears.

At Home With God

The death of my parents and the loss of the place I called "home" for 33 years have pushed me to strengthen my relationship with my Parent God. Becoming more and more at home with God is an ongoing process. It is not a straight path, and it does not erase the grief. However, since God is Creator and Parent of us all, coming home to God is a very natural journey. The journey home to God is described so well in the Parable of the Prodigal in Luke 15: 11-32. Centuries before Jesus told the parable others clearly affirmed God as their true home.

The eternal God is your refuge,
And underneath are the everlasting arms . . .
Deuteronomy 33: 27a

Lord, you have been our
dwelling place
in all generations.
Before the mountains were
brought forth,
or ever you had formed the
earth and the world,
from everlasting to everlasting
you are God.
Psalm 90: 1-2

Jack-in-the-Box

I'm not the one who died,
But I feel just half alive.
My emotions range from
Shredded to brittle.
Grief is exhausting work.
A news item on the television
Brought flooding memories.
Tears blurred my vision,
And I shook with sobs.
When will my memories
Lose their "jack-in-the-box" effect?

Caught By Surprise

More than a year after my mother died I moved to a city 50 miles from the town where I grew up. My parents had lived in that town for 36 years. My mother had moved away shortly after my father's death.

I did not realize that news from my hometown, Fort Pierce, Florida, would now be a part of local news on television and in the newspaper. The first time I watched the local news and heard a report about my hometown, grief flooded me. There I was watching the news and crying inconsolably. After years of living much farther away I was finally just an hour's drive from my old home, but it was not home any more. My parents were not there. They both had died.

My emotions, like a tightly wound jack-in-the-box, caught me by surprise. How unfair it was that I could not take a short drive to see my parents! What good was it to live that near if I could not drop in for a visit?

Grief is very hard work. It does not follow a clear, straight path. There are steep mountains and low valleys, twists and turns and times of doubling back over ground already covered. Sometimes the terrain is flooded with tears, and other times it is bone dry.

I had not expected to have to deal with a fresh layer of grief when I moved, but there it was. I acknowledged to myself, to God and to a close friend how intense my grief still was. Little by little I became used to hearing familiar places and names on the news and moved a few more steps along the healing path.

The prophet Ezekiel's "Valley of the Dry Bones" was a prophecy concerning the people of Israel. The prophetic words of new life and hope for Israel can also speak to our dry and brittle times. If God can revive a nation, then certainly God can breathe new life and hope into us.

The hand of the Lord came upon me, and he brought me out by the spirit of the Lord and set me down in the middle of a valley; it was full of bones. He led me all around them; there were very many lying in the valley, and they were very dry. He said to me, "Mortal, can these bones live?" I answered, "O Lord God, you know." Then he said to me, "Prophesy to these bones, and say to them: O dry bones, hear the word of the Lord. Thus says the Lord God to these bones: I will cause breath to enter you, and you shall live. I will lay sinews on you, and will cause flesh to come upon you, and cover you with skin and put breath in you, and you shall live; and you shall know that I am the Lord."

Ezekiel 37: 1-6

Merciful God, I feel scattered, dried up and drained of energy. Sometimes I even feel out of joint with your Spirit, unable to move, lifeless. I seek your breath of life. Fill me with your Spirit, O God, so that what has felt dead and dry and scattered may become alive in Christ. Call me away from the tombs of despair. Revive my faith and hope through your life giving love. Amen.

One More Time

Like thick, green puss
And living blood
The anger, fear,
And bitter loss
Burst, oozed and spurted
Out of her
Opening the wound
To healing,
One more time.

A Mix of Emotions

Sometimes the emotions of grief may overlap and mix together so that it is difficult to see where one ends and the other begins. At other times sadness may swallow up the anger, or anger overpower the sadness. Fear also may play "Hide and Seek." Recognizing that grief is a mixture of emotions makes it less disconcerting to experience the roller coaster ride of grief.

Creator, Life giver and Source of all that is, Word made flesh, Teacher, Healer, Redeemer of the world, Enlivening Spirit, Comforter, Counselor, Strength, only the breadth and depth of who you are can encompass the breadth and depth of my grief. Lift me from this murky fog into your renewing light. Amen.

Thick Silence

I never would have guessed
How painful silence is.
The house is so quiet
That I jump
When the refrigerator comes on.
All those busy,
Noisy years
When the house
Was full of lively family,
I yearned for
A little quiet time;
But I never wished for this.
Silence is thick.
I breathe it
And hear
The beating of my aching heart.
Speak to me, O God,
In this heavy silence.
Let me know I'm not alone
In this quiet, empty house.

At a time when the prophet Elijah felt utterly alone God's presence was made known to him in "the sound of sheer silence."

He said, "Go out and stand on the mountain before the Lord, for the Lord is about to pass by." Now there was a great wind, so strong that it was splitting mountains and breaking rocks in pieces before the Lord, but the Lord was not in the wind; and after the wind an earthquake; but the Lord was not in the earthquake; and after the earthquake a fire, but the Lord was not in the fire; and after the fire a sound of sheer silence. 1 Kings 19: 11-12

CHAPTER III

REMEMBERING AND CELEBRATING

Remembering and Celebrating

Over the years of my ministry I have led worship for many funerals and memorial services. It is always a privilege to hear the memories and celebrate a life. As I listen to the stories about the persons who have died, I look for the places where each person's story intersects with God's story. I look for scriptures that express those links. Death may not seem quite so strange and alien if it is seen in light of how God works in the midst of dying and in spite of death. If our stories are woven into God's story, then resurrection must be woven into our stories too.

Here is one way of expressing it.

Celebration of a Life

Precious in the sight of the Lord is the death of his saints. Ps 116; 15

A baby develops inside the mother's womb for approximately nine months. There are eyes but they cannot see. There is a nose, but it cannot smell. We know the arms and legs are moving, but they are far from grasping and holding things, far from walking. In the unborn stage the human fetus is beautifully intricate, yet far from fulfilling all she will become.

After approximately nine months we die to that stage of existence, and we are born into this present one. We begin to see a light and blink at it. We hear a voice that is more familiar than others and we coo at it. We start to crawl, walk, run, jump, and climb. We begin to reason and to think creatively. All of these capabilities that were seemingly unneeded in our first stage of existence now come into their full fruition and use.

I doubt if any of us would like to return to the darkness of our mother's womb. This life, with all of its problems and struggles, is far superior to that first stage of life. Likewise, our death to this stage of our existence allows us a birth into another stage that is of even greater dimension.

So it is that we come not to dwell on Janet's death but on her birth—her birth into everlasting life.

It has been hard for all those who loved and cared for Janet to watch over these past few months the labor pains for this birth. Her pain, her struggle, was intense. Yet, with the psalmist she could say, "I kept my faith, even when I said, 'I am greatly afflicted.'" Psalm 116: 10. In spite of the intensity of the physical struggle and the emotional roller coaster it put her loved ones on, all along the outcome of the truly decisive battle was already known. Through Christ the ultimate battle had already been won.

Described by her closest friends as a "Prayer Warrior," Janet would stay up until all hours of the night to pray with someone and to try to help that person. She prayed for so may people. In this final struggle innumerable people were praying for her, praying for her health, praying for her life.

Janet's death was not a "No" to our prayers. It was the ultimate "Yes!" Like a beautiful rainbow after a treacherous storm, peace, wholeness and eternal life have come.

A few months ago Janet and I discovered that we have the same birthday, June 29. We began to make plans to celebrate together. However, she has reached her birthday first, and I celebrate for her. We are all here to celebrate and remember.

Following Jesus' death and resurrection the disciples gathered and remembered. On the road to Emmaus Cleopas and his fellow traveler were talking and remembering. How clear were Jesus' instructions at the Last Supper that his followers remember him. We remember him when the stories of our lives are woven in with Jesus' story, God's great story of salvation. Therefore, it is appropriate that we remember Janet and some of the special ways in which her life was woven in with this great story.

Sharing of special memories.

Memories of Janet will bring smiles, laughter and tears in the days and years ahead. However, our memories would bring small comfort and little hope if they were all we had. In truth, it is not Janet's courage, sense of humor, special talents, love of family, loyalty to friends, or service to the community that give us hope at this hour. Rather, it is Christ's love and loyalty to Janet and her response to that love which give us hope. To God be the praise for the victory over death which is ours through Jesus Christ.

Prayer of Thanksgiving and Comfort

Eternal God, we come before you this day awed by the mysteries of life. As we celebrate the life of Janet, we give thanks that all of life is in your hands—birth, life as we know it, death and eternal life with you. You are always with us to guide, sustain, rejoice, comfort and even to ache with us through the various stages of life's journey. We give thanks for your sustaining power in Janet's life, for the faith out of which she served you through the church and in the community.

How wise you are, O God, in your plan that we have families to love, nurture, support and care for each other. Surround Janet's whole family with your comfort and your peace. Draw them close to each other and close to you. Guide us as a church family and as friends, that we may share our love in helpful and sensitive ways.

Most of all today we celebrate Christ, whose life, death and resurrection are the foundation of our hope, yes, even our joy in the midst of loss. He who fully understands suffering, pain and death has gone before us to prepare a place for us and has left with us a Comforter that we might not be alone. To God be the glory now and forever. Amen.

Mama

(Given to Mama for Christmas a year before she died)

Mama remembered
Watching her mother sew
The pretty dresses made for others,
Listening to the opera
With her Grandma
On Saturday afternoon,
Overhearing music lessons
Given by her aunt.
Her appreciation far exceeded
The meager opportunity
For her to play or sing.
Copying fashionable designs,
Mama played with patterns
'Til her daughters' dresses
Had a similar flair.
Dollar dresses
Made with so much care
Took me through
High school, college and beyond.
She would not call herself
An artist,
But she had the artistic eye.
Yards and yards of slipcovers
Made so things would match,
Food attractively arranged
On platter and on plate,
A shake of paprika or a parsley sprig
Was the completing touch.
Pinching pennies so
One daughter could have music lessons

The other art,
She encouraged us to stretch beyond
What pennies could afford.
Classical records,
Bought one a week
At A & P,
Library visits without limit,
Broadened the visions
And the dreams.

She would not call herself
Artist, musician, poet,
But she has been a vessel of both arts and crafts
For children, grandchildren,
And the ones for whom
She was their "other Mom."

(I added the day she died:)

Mama, you've gone home now
To God and many you loved,
But your light shines on
In those whose lives you touched.
With your sincere caring
And a gentle smile
You have taught us how to love
Even through great pain.
You have been a teacher.
You have taught us well,
To care and share in thankfulness,
In faith, in hope, in love.

Nana

Nana was an artist.
Her violin sang sweetly in her youth.
She painted fine china with soft designs,
With roses delicate as spring
And strawberries good enough to eat.
Designing patterns,
She made dresses for rich women
To feed her family during the Depression.
From flour sacks
She clothed her own children,
And patched together aprons
To protect the few dresses
She squeezed out for herself.
For her grandchildren
She tatted lace
For Peter Pan collars and small handkerchiefs.
A quilt was cut for each grandchild,
And an afghan started,
Still doll-size when she died.
Her violin and paint brush were
Untouched after her children's birth.
Yet, here and there among descendants
There is an artist eye, a musician's ear,
A poet who weaves an inherited melody
With images of present, past,
And yet to come.

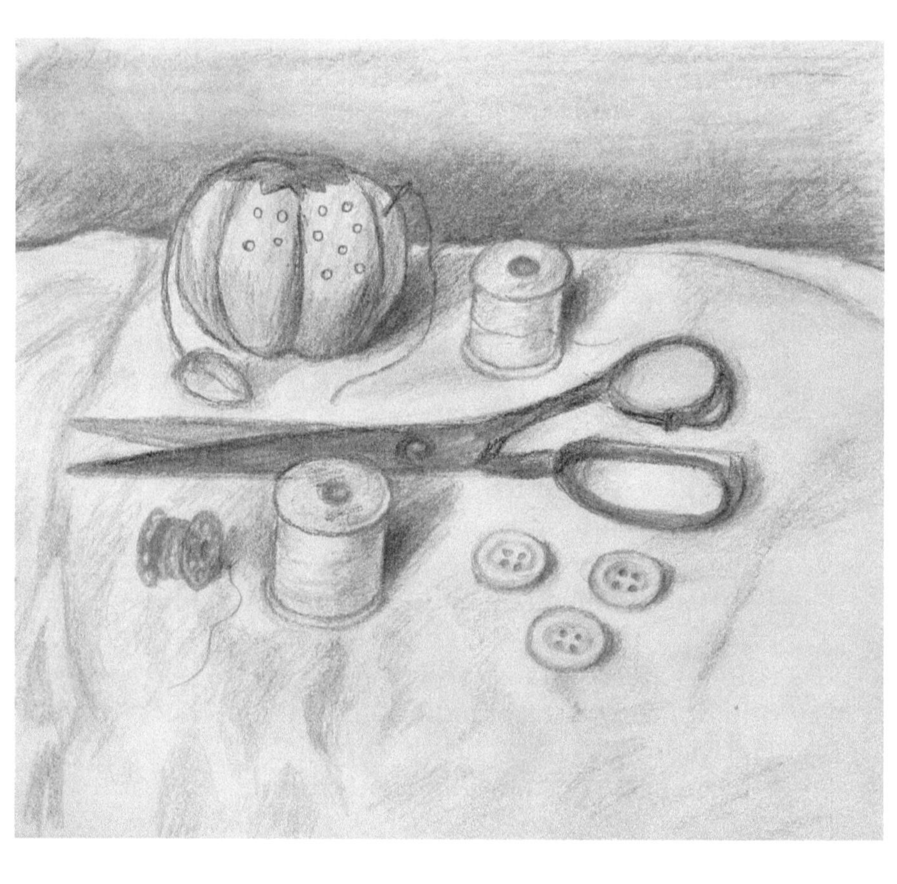

Remembering and Honoring

Remembering and honoring are parts of grieving. This may begin as a part of saying good-bye before the loved one dies and be continued after the death. Funerals and memorial services are an important part of this but they do not complete the process. It helps to reflect on the death and to share those reflections and memories of the one who has died with people who care about you.

By sharing family stories the legacy of those who have died continues to enrich the family. Whether we choose to live a very different life than those who went before or to follow closely in their footsteps, our family stories inform who we are. Telling the family stories not only helps preserve the unique history of the family, but it also aids the healing after a death.

Find Ways to Remember

Families come in so many different configurations now. One may not even be informed when a former in-law is dying. Nevertheless, if there was a significant relationship with that person grief will jump across the miles and years and reveal the depth of loss. It is important to acknowledge the grief for this person who touched your life in a special way. Even if family circumstances or distance prevents you from visiting the person before death or attending the funeral or memorial service you can set aside a time and place for remembering what that person meant to you. Share some of your special memories with a family member or friend. You may want to plant a tree or make a charitable donation in memory of this person. Find ways that are significant to you to honor this person and the relationship you had.

Mother "B"

(My Mother-in-law)

There was hardly time
To mourn you.
Mama was so sick
My grieving quickly
Turned to her.
I flew a lot of miles that year.
One trip was to you.
I said, "I love you, and
'Good-bye.'"—until we meet in heaven.
Your once large frame
So shrunken—
I did not think
You could become so small.
You still knew what you wanted
And what you didn't want.
Drinking in my presence,
My touch,
My words of thankfulness
And love,
Tightening your lips against
The moisture of a tiny sponge.
Do you know
I miss you?

Arriving full of smiles and hugs
With a boiled dinner in a pot,
And your famous apple pie.
Grandma Kay is here!
What a happy day!
Your eyes and those of your grandchildren
Sparkling with the same delight.
I know it broke your heart
When your son and I divorced.
Yet our love,
Yours and mine,
"Mother-in-love" and
"Daughter-in-love,"
Remained strong.
I felt it
As I saw you lying there,
Our bond
Sealed for eternity,
My precious Mother "B."

CHAPTER IV

ON THE SIDE OF LIGHT: STARTING TO HEAL

On the Side of Light

Between hurt and hope
I waiver, God,
Wresting with loss.
Yet with a simple song,
A friend's kind word,
A flower by the road,
A sunset tinged in gold,
A promised prayer,
You place your weight
On balance scale,
And ground it
On the side of light.

The people who walked in darkness
have seen a great light
those who live in a land of deep darkness—
on them light has shined.
Isaiah 9: 2

Thank you, God, for all the little rays of light you give to me in such simple ways. Slowly you push back the darkness until hope is born. Amen.

God Has Rocked Me

God has held me and rocked me,
God has cradled and calmed me.
God has stilled me and strengthened me.
God has blown through me like the wind
Through the oak trees
I have watched for hours,
And I am confident that
God will stretch
My withered wings
And give me power to fly.

Healing Pictures of God

Many people begin almost every prayer by addressing God with the name of a parent. Yet how many of us expect that God will treat us with the same intimate, tender care a loving parent gives to a troubled, hurting child?

As Jesus looked upon Jerusalem shortly before his arrest and crucifixion he agonized as a parent would for a child. There had been such a long history of pain, destruction and sorrow in the city; and his death would soon be added to the list. Not only for himself, but also for the people of Jerusalem, Jesus ached over what was to come. Like a mother weeping on behalf of her child, he cries out.

"Jerusalem, Jerusalem, the city that kills the prophets and stones those who are sent to it! How often have I desired to gather your children together as a hen gathers her brood under her wings, and you were not willing!" Matthew 23: 37.

When pain was great and energy very limited sometimes my prayer image of God's holding me, cradling and rocking me was the only thing which would bring me some relief and sleep.

The images of God in Scripture are many and very diverse. Explore them. Try praying with a different picture of God. Draw on the breadth and depth of God for the comfort, strength, solace and support you need.

Wind and Word, Shepherd, Physician, Comforter, Confronter, Holy God, you come to us and meet us in so may different ways: sometimes in a brief interlude of quietness in the busy whirl of our lives; sometimes in the midst of struggle, pain and heavy responsibilities. You reach out to us through the lives of those who have lived long and experienced much. You touch us through the amazing moments of creativity and birth. Meet us now as we long for healing and hope. Comfort and heal us and make us healers, too. Stretch us beyond ourselves and our sorrows to share with others Christ's powerful, transforming love. Amen.

The Fourth of July

It's a holiday,
And I'm alone.
Wistfully, I remember
Family picnics on the patio.
Mama went in and out with food
While Daddy tended the grill.
The children squirted each other
With the garden hose,
And my sister and I tried
To keep the picnic table dry.
With heat in the 90's
And bugs ready to attack the food,
We spent the Fourth of July
Together, long ago.
All are scattered now.
Daddy and Mama rest
In graves on the hill.
My children are grown
And far away.
My sister is cooking
For her own grandchildren.
My nieces chase the children
As we once did.
After a visit to my favorite antique shops
And an afternoon lost in a good book,
I watch fireworks on television
And tearfully sing "The Star Spangled Banner"
For no one else to hear.

Holidays, Birthdays and Anniversaries

Holidays, birthdays and anniversaries can be especially hard after a loss. Even if these times were not completely happy in the past there is still grief in the loss. Traditional symbols and activities, familiar food or just the opposite, the lack of the old familiar patterns, can trigger waves of grief. Recognizing that these can be difficult, emotional times and making some special plans can help. What aspects of past celebrations are most important to you? How might you continue to honor them? You may want to start some new traditions, visit with friends, or do something you love to do by yourself. Even though sadness may still creep into your day, it will be less likely to overwhelm you.

Compassionate God, I thank you for the assurance that you are with me. Whether I come to you sorrowing or celebrating you listen and care. Your steadfast love grounds me and your beckoning Spirit guides my movement and decisions. Touch the aching emptiness in my heart with your healing and empowering touch. Break through the dry ground of my grief with blooms of hope and joy. Amen.

Beyond Survival

The first rays of life beyond survival
Turn the tear-like dew
Into a million drops of light.
Hope dawns as clouds disperse.
I smile and laugh.

I will extol you, O Lord, for you
have drawn me up,
and did not let my foes rejoice
over me.
O Lord, my God, I cried to you
for help,
and you have healed me.
O Lord, you brought up my soul
from Sheol,
restored me to life from among
those gone down to the Pit.

You have turned my mourning
into dancing;
you have taken off my sackcloth
and clothed me with joy,
so that my soul may praise you
and not be silent.
O Lord my God, I will give
Thanks to you forever.
Psalm 30: 1-3, 11-12

Something New

In our grief we tend to focus on the past, on who and what we have lost. We resist the drastic changes that have come in our lives. We do not want something new. We want to retrieve what we had, our loved one, and the familiarity of our relationship with everything that accompanied it.

In spite of our resistance, God is able to bring something new and good out of loss. When Jerusalem was destroyed in the sixth century B.C. and the people of Israel were in exile, the prophet Ezekiel spoke words of hope even before there were signs of restoration.

A new heart I will give you, and a new spirit I will put within you; and I will remove from your body the heart of stone and give you a heart of flesh
Ezekiel 36: 26

Rays of Hope

Sunlight Filtering Through the trees
In the early morn,
Rays of hope dispersing the mists
The longer I sit still
The more images I see.
Images of a marred vessel
Being remolded,
A pot—punched down and rethrown.

In Isaiah 64 the prophet cried out to God to come with great power as in days past. In our grief we may call upon God for acts of power and miracles. We may even spew our anger all over God. Nothing we might say to God is beyond what God can handle. Just a quick look at the psalms and prophets will show that there is no request or complaint that God has not already heard.

After the prophet had made his strong plea to God, he recognized who he and all of God's people were in relation to God.

> "*Yet, O Lord, you are our Father,*
> *we are the clay, and you are our potter;*
> *we are all the work or your hand.*" Isaiah 64: 8

The healing of the wounds of grief happens slowly. No longer does grief consume every moment. Gradually we begin to notice the slivers of light filtering through the forest of grief. We will never be the same as we were before our loss. God, the potter, is able to work with us to shape our lives into new, beautifully unique and useful vessels.

Give Me a Sunrise

Give me a sunrise, O God,
Give me a sunrise.
Give me a sunrise, O God.
I need a sunrise in my soul.
Wash me in pinks and purples
And bright, white gold.
Grow within me, pushing back the clouds
Until You burst forth in light.

I have walked in heaviness
With leaden weights across my back, tied to my wrists and ankles,
Hung around my neck,
Each step methodical and slow,
Climbing up a down escalator
Into thick fog.
But I have seen you lift the
Clouds off mountains, God,
And dry the tear-like drops
From a single, fragile leaf.
I have seen hydrangeas weighted to the ground
Lift blooms again resiliently.
I have seen myself, back bent,
Eyes stained with red—
And felt you stretch me Tall,
Walking beside me up the aisle,
Touching me within a friend's firm clasp.
Behold, You have put your cross around my neck
And it is light.
Fill me with sunrise, O God,
And with the women of the Garden Dawn
I'll run and tell.

Ground of Hope

The story of the women at the garden tomb hearing of Jesus' resurrection and running to tell the good news has long empowered my life and ministry. That dawn and that news are the ground of our hope in spite of loss and grief.

After the sabbath, as the first day of the week was dawning, Mary Magdalene and the other Mary went to see the tomb. And suddenly there was a great earthquake; for an angel of the Lord, descending from heaven, came and rolled back the stone and sat on it. His appearance was like lightning, and his clothing white as snow. For fear of him the guards shook and became like dead men. But the angel said to the women, "Do not be afraid; I know that you are looking for Jesus who was crucified. He is not here; for he has been raised, as he said. Come, see the place where he lay. Then go quickly and tell his disciples, 'He has been raised from the dead, and indeed he is going ahead of you to Galilee; there you will see him.' This is my message for you." So they left the tomb quickly with fear and great joy and ran to tell his disciples. Matthew 28: 1-8

Living God, in awe and wonder I praise you. Christ is risen! The news that the women took from the empty tomb has broken through my grief. You have overpowered death and turned "mourning" into "morning". Days of endless gray give way to glints of gold. Healing and hope begin to grow. Thank you for this gift of renewed life. Amen.

A Different Dawn

Dawn feels different
After lengthy grief.
There is more texture
To the shadows,
And the warmth of day
Takes longer to penetrate
The layers of chilly loss.
Yet surely as it sets,
The sun comes up again.
Long hesitating spring
Asserts its right to bloom,
Proclaiming in fragrance and hue
The wonder of life anew.

www.ingramcontent.com/pod-product-compliance
Ingram Content Group UK Ltd.
Pitfield, Milton Keynes, MK11 3LW, UK
UKHW041924190726
13854UKWH00003B/1431

9 781453 576786